WHO WOULD WIN?®

RATTLESNAKE

VS.

SECRETARY BIRD

BY
JERRY PALLOTTA

ILLUSTRATED BY
ROB BOLSTER

Scholastic Inc.

The publisher would like to thank the following for their kind permission to use their photographs in this book:

Page 4 top: Brent Flint/Dreamstime; 4 center top: dfikar/Fotolia; 4 center bottom: Claire Fulton Dreamstime; 4 bottom: lucaar/Fotolia; 5 top: 7activestudio/Fotolia; 5 center top: Mike Neale Dreamstime; 5 center bottom: betweenthelines/Fotolia; 5 bottom: gregg williams/Fotolia; 6: Audrey Snider-Bell/Shutterstock, Inc.; 12: Courtesy Kyle Shepherd/Louisville Zoo; 13: Dan Porges/Getty Images; 18: John Cancalosi/Media Bakery; 19: Panoramic Images/Getty Images 20 center: Don Juan Moore/AP Images; 21 bottom left: Robertosch/Dreamstime; 21 bottom right Robertosch/Dreamstime.

To Grace Stevenson, who loves to read!
— J. P.

To Charlie, Eddie, Bobby D., and Ted, who love to learn!
— R. B.

Text copyright © 2016 by Jerry Pallotta.
Illustrations copyright © 2016 by Rob Bolster.

All rights reserved. Published by Scholastic Inc., *Publishers since 1920.* SCHOLASTIC and associated logos are trademarks and/or registered trademarks of Scholastic Inc.

The publisher does not have any control over and does not assume any responsibility for author or third-party websites or their content.

No part of this publication may be reproduced, stored in a retrieval system, or transmitted in any form or by any means, electronic, mechanical, photocopying, recording, or otherwise, without written permission of the publisher. For information regarding permission, write to Scholastic Inc., Attention: Permissions Department, 557 Broadway, New York, NY 10012.

ISBN 978-0-545-68115-5

20 19 18 17 16 15 14 13 12   18 19 20

Printed in the U.S.A.   40
First printing 2016

Book design by Rob Bolster and Jerry Pallotta

The rattlesnake is hungry and is looking for a bird to eat. What bird should it go after? If it attacks a bird, who would win?

BIRDS OF PREY

Should the rattlesnake attack an osprey? This ocean bird eats by catching fish with its sharp talons.

NAME FACT
Ospreys are also called sea hawks.

A bald eagle? It is a national symbol of the United States of America.

FACT
You can find it on a one-dollar bill.

A barn owl? It eats mice, voles, shrews, and other small mammals.

STEALTH FACT
An owl's feathers are shaped so it can fly quietly.

A vulture? Not a pretty bird. It eats carrion.

DEFINITION
Carrion is the rotten body of a dead animal.

OTHER BIRDS

A peacock? What beautiful tail feathers! This bird is in the pheasant family.

> **CORRECT TERMS**
> *A male is a peacock.*
> *A female is a peahen.*

A wild turkey? Sorry, turkey!

A sandhill crane? It looks like a dinosaur with feathers.

> **SOUND FACT**
> *Sandhill cranes squawk so loud you can hear them miles away.*

A hummingbird? No! Too small!

> **SIZE FACT**
> *A hummingbird egg is the size of an M&M.*

None of these birds look interesting enough! How about a secretary bird? What a strange name. We'll meet it soon.

The western diamondback rattlesnake is a venomous snake found in North America. Its scientific name is *Crotalus atrox*. Its name means "fierce rattle."

NAME FACT

Repeated sheddings of its skin creates a rattle at the end of its tail. When threatened, this snake rattles its tail.

DANGER

Venomous means having a poisonous bite.

You can identify different rattlesnakes by the designs on their scales. Do you see the diamond skin pattern?

MEET THE SECRETARY BIRD

The secretary bird lives in Africa. Its scientific name is *Sagittarius serpentarius*. It has an unusual diet—it eats snakes and other animals.

STARRY NAME

Its scientific name comes from two constellations: Sagittarius, *which means archer, and* serpentarius, *which means serpent handler.*

FACT

Birds don't have arms and hands; they have wings.

DEFINITION

A constellation is a pattern of stars in the sky that makes a shape.

Its head looks like it is surrounded by quill pens. That's how it got the name secretary bird.

LENGTH

The western diamondback rattlesnake can grow up to about 7 feet long. Here are silhouettes of a basketball player and a rattlesnake.

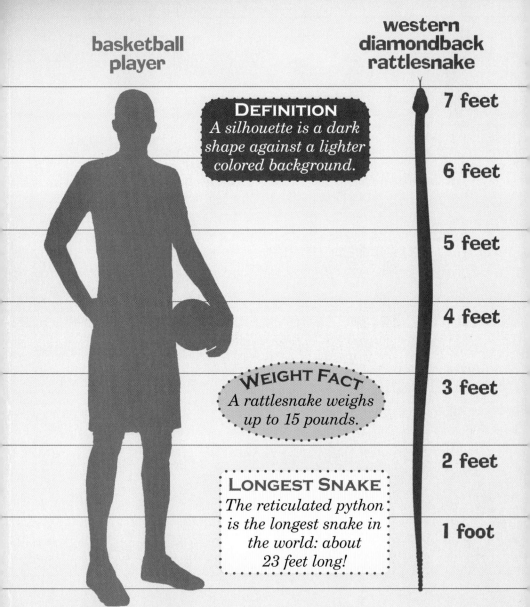

basketball player

western diamondback rattlesnake

DEFINITION
A silhouette is a dark shape against a lighter colored background.

7 feet

6 feet

5 feet

4 feet

WEIGHT FACT
A rattlesnake weighs up to 15 pounds.

3 feet

2 feet

LONGEST SNAKE
The reticulated python is the longest snake in the world: about 23 feet long!

1 foot

If you hear the rattle, stay away! It's not the biggest or the smallest snake. But it is a deadly, venomous snake.

HEIGHT

For a bird, it's really tall. A secretary bird can grow up to 4 feet high. That's taller than most kindergartners.

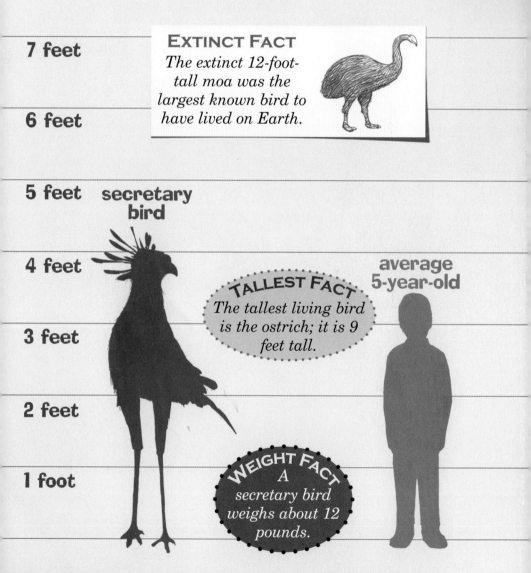

7 feet

EXTINCT FACT
The extinct 12-foot-tall moa was the largest known bird to have lived on Earth.

6 feet

5 feet   **secretary bird**

4 feet   **average 5-year-old**

TALLEST FACT
The tallest living bird is the ostrich; it is 9 feet tall.

3 feet

2 feet

WEIGHT FACT
A secretary bird weighs about 12 pounds.

1 foot

Most of its height is in its legs. Long, skinny legs!

IT'S A REPTILE

A reptile is a cold-blooded vertebrate animal that is covered in dry scales or horny plates. Snakes, lizards, crocodilians, and turtles are reptiles.

DID YOU KNOW?
Vertebrate means an animal with a spinal cord.

FACT
Most reptiles lay eggs.

FACT
Snakes have scales.

The rattlesnake has a forked tongue. Its tongue is multitalented; it can taste, smell, and tell temperature.

IT'S A BIRD

Birds are warm-blooded, winged vertebrates that are covered in feathers, and have scaly legs, and a beak.

GROUNDED FACT
Kiwis, penguins, kakapos, chickens, ostriches, emus, cassowaries, elephant birds, and rheas cannot fly.

BORING FACT
The secretary bird does not have a special tongue.

NO-TEETH FACT
Birds have beaks, not teeth.

RATTLESNAKE SKELETON

This is a rattlesnake skeleton. Ribs, ribs, and more ribs!
What does the skeleton remind you of?

a. *coiled spring*
b. *Slinky*
c. *dragon*
d. *all of the above*

NUMBER FACT
Humans have 33 vertebrae and 12 sets of ribs.

ANOTHER NUMBER
Rattlesnakes have between 200 and 400 vertebrae and ribs!

FACT
Snakes have teeth called fangs.

SECRETARY BIRD SKELETON

This is the skeleton of a secretary bird. What does it remind you of? Does it look like a dinosaur skeleton?

NICKNAMES
African Marching Eagle, Serpent Eagle, and the Devil's Horse.

KNEE FACT
Most birds, including the secretary bird, have knees that bend backward.

FIND ME

Western diamondback rattlesnakes live mostly in western North America. Here is where they live.

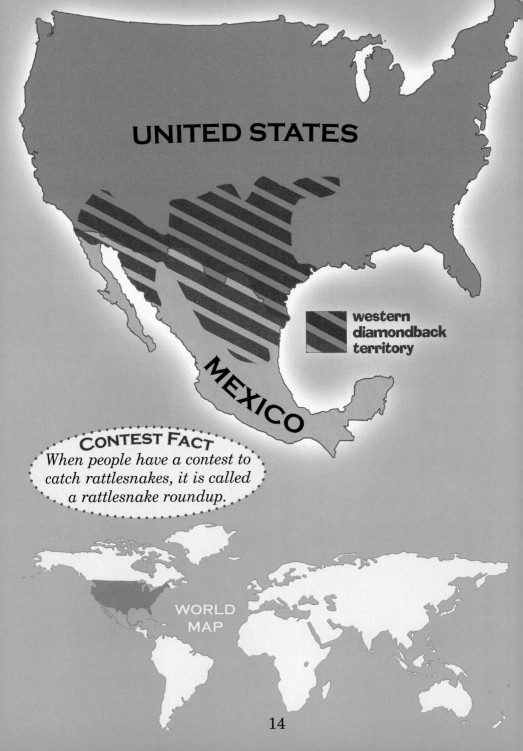

UNITED STATES

MEXICO

western diamondback territory

CONTEST FACT

When people have a contest to catch rattlesnakes, it is called a rattlesnake roundup.

WORLD MAP

LOOK FOR ME

The secretary bird lives in the grassy plains and savannahs of Africa.

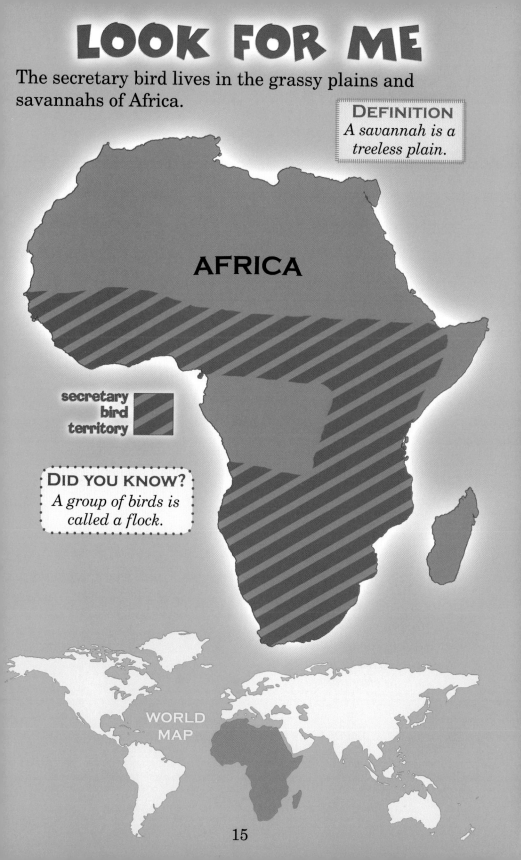

DEFINITION
A savannah is a treeless plain.

AFRICA

secretary bird territory

DID YOU KNOW?
A group of birds is called a flock.

WORLD MAP

WHAT'S SPECIAL?

What is special about rattlesnakes? Rattles!

FACT
*The rattle is at the tail
end of the snake.*

DID YOU KNOW?
*A rattlesnake is not
the type of snake to go
looking for trouble. The
rattle sound is a warning
to stay away.*

Rattlesnakes molt and shed their skin. The more times
they shed, the longer their rattles.

WHAT'S UNIQUE?

What is special about secretary birds? They have the longest legs of any bird of prey. Their lower legs are extra skinny. This protects the secretary bird, because there is nothing there for a snake to bite.

DID YOU KNOW?
Ornithology is the scientific study of birds.

COUNTING FACT
Birds have four toes on each foot.

Their toes are as sharp as razor blades. Watch out—they kick, they stomp! They even kick snakes.

DELICIOUS

Rattlesnakes prefer to eat small mammals. This rattlesnake is eating a mouse.

Rattlesnakes eat rabbits, rats, voles, mice, squirrels, gerbils, prairie dogs, chipmunks, and hamsters.

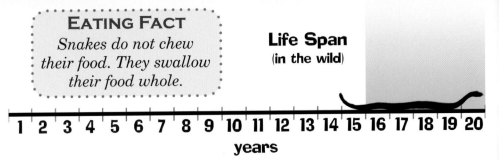

EATING FACT
Snakes do not chew their food. They swallow their food whole.

Life Span
(in the wild)

1 2 3 4 5 6 7 8 9 10 11 12 13 14 15 16 17 18 19 20
years

Rattlesnakes have no interest in eating humans. People are too big for them. Rattlesnakes eat only what they can swallow whole. They also eat frogs, birds, lizards, and other snakes.

YUMMY

The secretary bird eats snakes and lizards. When they find snakes, they kick them with their razor-sharp claws. Whap! Whap! Whap! They also attack with their sharp beaks.

Here is a secretary bird eating a lizard. It looks delicious! Can you imagine eating a live lizard?

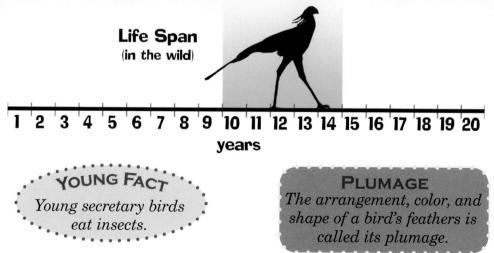

Life Span
(in the wild)

1 2 3 4 5 6 7 8 9 10 11 12 13 14 15 16 17 18 19 20
years

YOUNG FACT
Young secretary birds eat insects.

PLUMAGE
The arrangement, color, and shape of a bird's feathers is called its plumage.

FAMOUS

There is a Major League Baseball team called the Arizona Diamondbacks.

FUN FACT
Snakes have dry skin; they are not greasy or slimy.

The Florida A&M Rattlers have a great logo on their helmet.

DEFINITION
An ophiologist is a scientist who studies snakes.

ODDBALL

Secretary bird is a strange name. Should it be renamed the soccer bird because of its kicking ability?

I can head the ball, too.

STRANGE
It is a unique bird. It has a face like an eagle, legs like a stork, and it eats like a bird of prey.

The secretary bird is the national symbol of Sudan. It's also on the coat of arms of South Africa.

SUDAN

SOUTH AFRICA

SLOW

Rattlesnakes move slowly. They slither up to 2 or 3 miles per hour.

SAFE FACT
Rattlesnakes can go underground to hide and be safe. Their home is called a den.

FUN FACT
A den is the home of a community of snakes. A burrow is the home of one snake.

HIDE LOW

DID YOU KNOW?
Up to 200 rattlesnakes can live in one den.

RUN

The secretary bird runs fast. It is considered a terrestrial bird. That means it mostly stays on the ground. It prefers to run.

SPEED LIMIT 20

DID YOU KNOW?
It can fly. But it takes a while to get off the ground.

SLEEP HIGH

At night, secretary birds fly high up in acacia trees and safely sleep. Lions, hyenas, and jackals can't get them in a tree.

WEAPONS

Rattlesnakes have fangs and poisonous venom. They bite and then inject the venom through the hollow fangs.

FACT
Rattlesnake venom is a coagulant. It ruins the lining of your cells.

When it attacks, it is lightning fast.

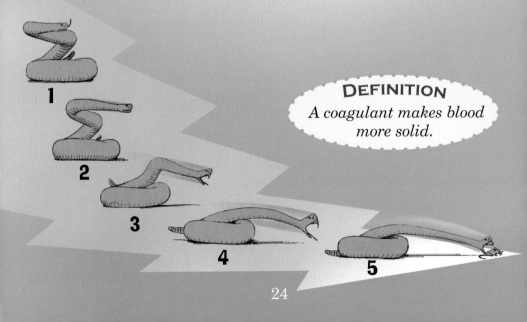

DEFINITION
A coagulant makes blood more solid.

1
2
3
4
5

WEAPONS

The secretary bird has four great weapons. It can fly, run fast, and has a sharp beak and deadly claws.

DEFINITION
A raptor is a bird that hunts and eats other animals.

It can jab with its beak, stomp with its feet, and kick with its long legs.

The secretary bird is in an acacia tree, ready to hunt. It's on the lookout. In the wild, it is eat or be eaten. The secretary bird looks down on the ground for food.

The rattlesnake is safe and sound in its den. It's getting hungry. It decides to take a peek outside.

The rattlesnake sticks its head out of its hole. It's looking for a tasty mouse or a delicious rat to eat. The secretary bird sees the snake, swoops down, and uses its feet to stomp the rattlesnake's head.

Ouch, that hurt! The snake wiggles back into its den.

Now the secretary bird is on the ground. It can fly, but it can also run fast. It looks around. Where did that snake go? The snake decides to fake out the bird and use its secret second escape tunnel.

RARE
Most raptors attack from the air; the secretary bird attacks on the ground.

The bird hears it. As the rattlesnake moves out of the den, the secretary bird uses its foot to stomp on the snake again

The snake moves into a defensive position to bite the bird. The secretary bird's body is too tall for the snake to reach. The snake tries to sink its fangs into the bird's ankle. But there isn't enough there to bite. The bird dances away.

The snake tries to bite again. Yikes! Poison! The bird has to be careful. The bird kicks the snake.Whap! Then the bird stomps on the snake with its razor-sharp claws.

Whap! The bird kicks the snake again. The snake goes flying in the air.

The snake lands on the ground. It decides to skip dinner and escape to its den.

As the snake moves back and forth across the ground, the secretary bird keeps on kicking it. Whap! Whap! Whap! In between kicks, the secretary bird pecks the snake on its head. Bop! The rattlesnake is wounded.

BALANCE FACT

The secretary bird uses its wings to balance itself while stomping on a snake.

The bird gives it another kick! Whap!

The secretary bird eats the rattlesnake. The fight is over. What must it be like to eat a wounded venomous snake? Yuck!

WHO HAS THE ADVANTAGE? CHECKLIST

RATTLESNAKE

SECRETARY BIRD

☐	Size	☐
☐	Venom	☐
☐	Claws	☐
☐	Legs	☐
☐	Flight	☐
☐	Speed	☐
☐	Tail	☐

Author's note: This is one way the fight might have ended. How would you write the ending?